I0762635

Over-the-Top Animals

Biggest Bird

By Suzane Nguyen

BLASTOFF! BEGINNERS, AN IMPRINT OF BELLWETHER MEDIA BY FLUTTERBEE

Blastoff! Beginners are developed by literacy experts and educators to meet the needs of early readers. These engaging informational texts support young children as they begin reading about their world. Through simple language and high frequency words paired with crisp, colorful photos, Blastoff! Beginners launch young readers into the universe of independent reading.

Sight Words in This Book

a	big	long	the	they
an	have	run	their	
are	help	see	them	
away	it	than	these	

This edition first published in 2027 by Bellwether Media, Inc.

For information regarding permission, write to Bellwether Media, Inc., Attention: Permissions Department, 3500 American Blvd W, Suite 150, Bloomington, MN 55431.

Library of Congress Cataloging-in-Publication Data is available at www.loc.gov or upon request from the publisher.

ISBN: 9798898800062 (hardcover)
ISBN: 9798898801427 (ebook)

Editor: Betsy Rathburn Designer: Laura Sowers

Printed in the United States of America, North Mankato, MN.

Table of Contents

An ostrich
sees danger.
It runs away fast!

Ostriches are the biggest birds!

They are tall.
They are taller
than a person!

They have big wings. The wings have long **feathers**.

feathers

They have
long legs.
Their feet have
sharp **claws**.

Staying Safe

Ostriches are strong. Their size helps them.

They cannot fly.
They run fast.
Big wings help
them **steer**.

They kick **predators**. Their claws hurt!

These big birds stay safe!

The Biggest Bird

Body Parts

Using Their Size

run fast

steer while running

kick predators

Glossary

sharp nails

the outer coverings of birds

animals that hunt other animals for food

to control movement

To Learn More

ON THE WEB

FACTSURFER

Factsurfer.com gives you a safe, fun way to find more information.

1. Go to www.factsurfer.com.
2. Enter "biggest bird" into the search box and click 🔍.
3. Select your book cover to see a list of related content.

Index

The images in this book are reproduced through the courtesy of: Krakenimages.com, front cover; Stock, pp. 3, 22; paula, pp. 4-5; sergei_fish13, pp. 6-7, 20-21; JENNIFER, pp. 8-9; Krzysztof Bubel, p. 10; Kathrin, pp. 10-11; thepoo, p. 12; Serge Goujon, pp. 12-13; EcoView, pp. 14-15, 16-17; Natalia, p. 18; Alain Mafart-Renodier/ Biosphoto, pp. 18-19; gi0572, p. 22 (run fast); JWCohen, p. 22 (steer while running); Zoonar GmbH/ Alamy Stock Photo, p. 22 (kick predators); schankz, p. 23 (claws); fotografie4you.eu, p. 23 (feathers); Dr Ajay Kumar Singh, p. 23 (predators); RomanR, p. 23 (steer).